SOME SUNNY DAY

SOME SUNNY DAY

A Play by
MARTIN SHERMAN

AMBER LANE PRESS

All rights whatsoever in this play are strictly reserved
and application for performance, etc., must be made
before rehearsals begin, to:
Casarotto Ramsay Ltd,
60-66 Wardour Street,
London W1V 4ND
No performance may be given unless a licence has
been obtained.

First published in 1996 by
Amber Lane Press Ltd,
Cheorl House, Church Street, Charlbury, Oxford OX7 3PR
Telephone and fax: 01608 810024

Printed in Great Britain
by The Guernsey Press Company, C.I.

ISBN 1 872868 18 5

Some Sunny Day was first presented at the
Hampstead Theatre, London, on 11th April 1996,
with the following cast
(in order of appearance):

ROBIN . . . Rupert Everett
ALEC . . . David Bark-Jones
HAMID . . . Eddy Lamar
HORATIO . . . Corin Redgrave
DUCHESS . . . Sara Kestelman
EMILY . . . Cheryl Campbell

Director . . . Roger Michell
Designer . . . Bill Dudley
Lighting Designer . . . Mark Henderson
Sound Designer . . . John A Leonard

ACT ONE

Cairo. July, 1942.

A large shabby flat near the British Embassy.

*A huge sitting room in a perpetual state of
chaos. Amongst the clutter are two sofas, several
wicker chairs, a kitchen table, a fridge, a phono-
graph, a large flowered screen, a grandfather
clock and a tall earthenware jar. Flowers and
fruit everywhere. Newspaper photographs of
King George and Queen Elizabeth and Winston
Churchill tacked onto the left wall.*

*A window at the right, with a view of the street
and lemon trees. A balcony on the left.*

*A hallway, upstage, leads into the sitting room.
The hallway is filled with uniform cases,
luggage, photographs, magazines, letters tied
with string, all piled together. A front door
opens from the street into the hallway. Several
other doors — to bedrooms — are glimpsed
opposite the front door.*

*It is 3 a.m. The sitting room is dark, but light
from the street — and the moon — pours in
from the window.*

ROBIN — *early thirties, somewhat other-worldly,
with a slight New Zealand accent — stares out
of the window. He wears a robe.*

ROBIN   [*sings*] "Twinkle, twinkle, little star,
How I wonder who you are . . . "
[*laughs*] Well, actually . . .

> [ALEC — *mid-twenties, rather upper class,
> has come in from the hallway. He wears
> a robe as well.*]

ALEC   What are you doing?

ROBIN   Shooting star. Look.

                [*He points to the sky.*]

ALEC   Where?

ROBIN   Missed it. They come and go.

ALEC   Like you.

ROBIN   Rather.

ALEC   Sky is red.

ROBIN   Bonfires. Embassies are still burning papers.
I'd write an article about it — news flash, you
know — city in panic — but the censors would
kill it, so I won't bother, what the hell — did
you know the American Embassy has loaded a
bunch of cars, ready for a getaway . . . ?

ALEC   Will you stop talking?

ROBIN   I'm nervous.

ALEC   I'm the chap who should be nervous, not you.
My leave is up in the morning — remember?

ROBIN   Yes.

ALEC   Jerries advancing. Rommel practically at our
door. What's needed . . .

ROBIN   Is what?

ALEC   *Me*. In the desert.

ROBIN   What would you do? Offer Rommel tea?

ALEC   Shoot someone, that's what. Lead charges. Do
something brave with a tank.

ROBIN   You're a child.

ALEC   I'm not meant to sit behind a desk.

ROBIN   [*upset*] No.

[ROBIN *points out of the window.*]

ROBIN　Look! There!

ALEC　Where?

ROBIN　Another one.

ALEC　I don't see . . .

ROBIN　I think. Unless it was just some damn fool planet that made a wrong turn. The traffic must be as bad in the sky as it is in Cairo.

ALEC　This might be our last night . . .

ROBIN　Don't you ever wonder?

ALEC　About what?

ROBIN　What's out there?

[ALEC *takes* ROBIN's *hand.*]

ALEC　No.

[ALEC *kisses* ROBIN.]

Come back to bed.

[*Blackout.*]

Cries from a minaret are heard. The muezzin calling men to morning prayer.

The lights rise. Early morning.

The room is bathed in light. Sounds of morning traffic and street-vendors. HAMID, *wearing a galabiya and a fez, sits on the floor, shuffling a deck of cards.*

HORATIO, *dapper but distracted, in his early fifties, enters the hallway from the front door. He walks into the sitting room.*

HORATIO　Hamid.

HAMID	Not so good.
HORATIO	What's not so good?
HAMID	Your cards.

[HORATIO *takes off his jacket.*]

HORATIO	Those are not my cards. Make yourself at home, why don't you?
HAMID	I see much danger.
HORATIO	You're terribly Sabu today, aren't you?
HAMID	You are in love.
HORATIO	Really? The cards say that?

[HORATIO *removes the lid of the earthenware jar and scoops a cup inside. The jar is filled with liquid. He sticks a finger into the cup, tastes it, winces, then drinks.*]

HAMID	All Cairo knows you are in love. Nothing to do with cards.
HORATIO	How does all Cairo know?
HAMID	Because you talk. Talk to everybody. Talk, talk, talk. [*pulls a card from the pack*] Ah — I see much trouble.
HORATIO	Hamid — go away.
HAMID	But you send for me.
HORATIO	Oh. Oh yes. Stupid stuff, actually. Look, here is a bit of money. [*removes a few bills from his pocket*] We would like you to . . .

[HAMID *takes the money.*]

HAMID	Tell people British will win. When I read fortunes.
HORATIO	How did you know?

HAMID   British pay all fortune-tellers in Cairo. I think maybe you forget about me. Must say Rommel will not enter city. All fortune-tellers must say this. This is how you win war.

HORATIO It *is* the truth.

HAMID   Then why you burn papers? [*removes a charred piece of paper from his pocket*] Look — top secret. Fall on my head. Pieces of paper falling all over Cairo. Raining paper.

HORATIO What is it?

HAMID   Food for lunch.

[HORATIO *takes the paper.*]

HORATIO Oh, dear, the Embassy menu.

HAMID   British eat too much in afternoon. Germans are more hungry.

HORATIO What did you mean — trouble?

HAMID   Trouble?

HORATIO In love.

HAMID   Oh. Hamid cannot answer, one, two, three. Have to do your cards proper. Take time.

HORATIO Haven't time. Anyhow, you're an outrageous fake.

HAMID   Only fake when British pay me to lie.

HORATIO OK, Hamid — that's enough — piss off . . .

HAMID   Not enough money to lie.

HORATIO I have hardly anything left.

[*He searches through his pockets, removes a wad of bills and hands them to* HAMID.]

Better?

[ROBIN *enters from the hallway.*]

ROBIN   Well, well, well. A spot of baksheesh? Salaam, Hamid.

HAMID   Salaam, my friend. I receive money to say Rommel stay in desert.

HORATIO   Hamid!

HAMID   You pay only for lie.

HORATIO   Bugger.

[*He removes another wad of bills and hands them to* HAMID.]

This is all there is.

HAMID   Good. Now I lie and don't tell anyone I lie. OK?

HORATIO   Yes, yes.

[HAMID *gathers the cards and rises.*]

HAMID   When you want to know about love and trouble, trouble and love, I sincerely read cards.

[HAMID *leaves.*]

ROBIN   [*cutting up an orange*] I declare — was that espionage?

HORATIO   If you like.

[*He dips his cup into the earthenware jar again.*]

ROBIN   How's the goula?

HORATIO   Not much grapefruit juice left. Lots of fake gin. [*drinks*] Ghastly. Still . . .

[*He holds out his cup to* ROBIN.]

ROBIN   Too early.

HORATIO   What we're doing, actually, is instigating a new whispering campaign. Fortune-tellers, beggars,

holy men, dwarfs, amputees — all spreading
false information throughout the city to diplo-
mats, soldiers, war correspondents, pashas,
emirs — you name it, every brand of Levantine
and Coptic riff-raff, who are busy spreading
their own equally fake information to whoever
will listen, which means everyone, everyone in
Cairo, even the King. It's what we boys in
Propaganda do, you know that. This is, of
course, off the record, which is a pity, it would
make an interesting article for you, assuming
you do write articles, assuming you are indeed
a reporter, assuming you have a byline in the
Auckland Herald, assuming you are from New
Zealand . . .

ROBIN   I'm not really. I'm from outer space.

HORATIO   Wouldn't surprise me. My instinct, my little
nose, tells me you're a liar, but then, who really
cares? I don't give a flying fuck, and you
certainly keep our landlord happy.

ROBIN   Well, assuming I am a reporter, you boys in
Propaganda won't let me file anything, will
you? This whole flap about Rommel perched in
the desert, making mincemeat of the Allies,
about to enter the city like Cleopatra, is
actually spectacular news. But it will never be
printed. Unless it's all true, and Cairo falls.
The Germans will be happy to get *that* news
out, I imagine.

> [*He starts picking from a bowl of fruit; he
> holds it out to* HORATIO.]

Figs? They're delicious. Anyway — this is all
assuming I am who I say I am. Never assume,
my beauty. And where exactly was the Prince
of Propaganda last night?

HORATIO   Officially — at the Embassy burning top secret
files.

ROBIN   Unofficially?

HORATIO   With Tahia.

ROBIN   Ummm . . .

HORATIO   Which is something I don't want to talk about.
            Actually, I am peckish.

            [ROBIN *holds out the fruit.*]

ROBIN   Grapes.

            [HORATIO *sits at the table.*]

HORATIO   Thanks. Because it's beyond the power of
            words.

ROBIN   What is?

HORATIO   What I won't talk about. It has nothing to do
            with anything as mundane as language. And,
            yes, I am perfectly aware that I have, in my
            time, used words, that I was a novelist of at
            least minor importance before this ridiculous
            war interrupted everything, but that world,
            that verbal world, has nothing to do with my
            life any more; what I'm trying to say is that I
            can't possibly say what I'm trying to say, do you
            see? I dare not begin to tell you how much she
            loves me. There. Your fevered disinterest has
            forced it out of me. She loves me. She loves me
            in a way that she has never loved before, she
            loves me as she has loved no one else.
            Sometimes — in the morning — her heart
            sings. I absolutely refuse to discuss this. But it
            is fascinating, isn't it? I'm very aware of that.
            I've never been . . . no . . . and now I'm . . . no
            . . . and to think, and certainly, at my age . . .
            oh no. No, no, I could not have dreamt of this. I
            could never have imagined that one day Cairo's
            most important belly dancer would love me so.

            [ROBIN *starts to giggle.*]

Why are you laughing?

ROBIN   Promise me one thing.

HORATIO   What?

ROBIN   Never make me read your novels.

HORATIO   This is not funny. She is actually a writer as well. Stop it. You see — every motion of the belly is in itself equivalent to a letter of the alphabet. She composes a song for me as she dances.

ROBIN   You read her hips?

HORATIO   You don't understand.

ROBIN   Actually, I rather wish you wouldn't tell me all this, as I am rather fond of your wife. Remember Emily, your wife?

HORATIO   You live in the past.

> [*The* DUCHESS *— mid-forties, with a look of grand impoverishment and a mid-European accent, rushes into the sitting room from the hallway.*]

DUCHESS   I cannot stand the streets! This country is too hot! And filled with flies. Insects! And sand — from the desert. The wind blows the sand.

ROBIN   Khamsin.

DUCHESS   What is that?

ROBIN   The desert wind.

DUCHESS   Yes, yes. My hair is filled with sand.

ROBIN   Gets inside the foreskin.

HORATIO   Please. I'm eating.

ROBIN   So the soldiers say. There's an Aussie medical officer out there performing circumcisions.

DUCHESS   There was a dead camel on the street.

HORATIO   Oh Christ.

          [*He pushes the fruit away.*]

DUCHESS   Little children were cutting the camel up for food.

ROBIN   You're not used to seeing such things, are you, Duchess?

DUCHESS   In Russia we never saw dead camel. Every so often — here and there — a dead person perhaps. Oh my God! The shit! The shit!

          [*The* DUCHESS *runs around the room in total panic.*]

ROBIN   What?

DUCHESS   A wasp! A wasp!

ROBIN   Where?

          [*The* DUCHESS *runs from the room and cowers in the hallway.* ROBIN *searches for a wasp.*]

HORATIO   Is she from outer space as well?

ROBIN   I think not.

HORATIO   She's an imposter.

ROBIN   Of course.

DUCHESS   [*from the hallway*] Is it gone?

ROBIN   I don't see a wasp.

          [*The* DUCHESS *ventures back into the sitting room.* HORATIO *returns to the fruit bowl. He dips pieces of fruit into a jar of honey.*]

DUCHESS   I do not like insects. I must leave this city. I must go to Palestine. There are no wasps in

Palestine. It is more civilized. But the trains are full. Even at this hour, at the station, people fight for space on a train. They are afraid of the Germans.

ROBIN Are you afraid of the Germans, Duchess?

DUCHESS It's the wasps I fear. At any rate there is no reason to worry. I went to Shalimar.

ROBIN Shalimar?

DUCHESS The fortune-teller. She said Germans will not enter Cairo. All the same, I must leave this city. I must have a pass for the train, Horatio.

HORATIO I'm eating, actually.

DUCHESS The train to Palestine.

HORATIO Have some kumquat.

DUCHESS The midnight train.

HORATIO Berries.

DUCHESS Only an embassy can produce a pass.

HORATIO They are not easy to come by.

DUCHESS Whoever helps a Grand Duchess will some day be considered a hero.

HORATIO We're up to our ass in duchesses, Duchess. There are princes and barons crawling all over our Embassy, trying to leave Cairo.

DUCHESS The shit! The shit! It is back!

[*The* DUCHESS *runs back into the hallway.*]

HORATIO [*to* ROBIN] Will you please kill the wasp?

ROBIN Don't be silly. They sting. There it is!

[ROBIN *flaps his arms in the air and runs over to the window. He closes the shut-*

> *ters. The room is darkened. He switches
> on the light and calls to the* DUCHESS.]

It flew out the window.

> [*The* DUCHESS *returns to the sitting
> room.*]

DUCHESS   Are you certain?

HORATIO   Have a banana. With honey.

DUCHESS   It is the honey that attracts them. There are no
insects in Palestine. That's why your ships go
there.

HORATIO   Pardon?

DUCHESS   Your ships.

HORATIO   Ships?

DUCHESS   Your fleet. They leave Alexandria. They sail to
Haifa.

HORATIO   How do you know that?

> [*The* DUCHESS *removes a charred piece of
> paper from her pocket and waves it at*
> HORATIO.]

DUCHESS   It fell on my head. [*unravels the paper and
reads*] Memorandum.

HORATIO   Damn.

DUCHESS   The wind from the desert. What do you call it?

ROBIN   Khamsin.

DUCHESS   Yes. List of ships. Officers of ships. A few
letters missing from the names, but a few
letters preserved.

HORATIO   I'll see what I can do.

DUCHESS   Please.

[*The* DUCHESS *flashes the paper at* HORA-TIO *again, then walks into the hallway and enters her bedroom.*]

HORATIO   Everyone knows about the fleet. It's hardly a secret.

ROBIN   I think she really needs a pass.

[ALEC *enters the sitting room.*]

HORATIO   [*to* ALEC] This house is filled with imposters.

ALEC   What?

HORATIO   You accept money from imposters.

ALEC   And where is yours?

HORATIO   My what?

ALEC   Your rent.

HORATIO   Oh. As a matter of fact . . .

ALEC   You spent it on the dancer. As a matter of fact.

[ALEC *untacks the photographs of King George, Queen Elizabeth and Winston Churchill from the wall. There is a bullseye underneath, complete with bullet holes.*]

ROBIN   I wish you wouldn't do that.

[ALEC *opens a drawer in the kitchen table and removes a pistol.*]

ALEC   Practice.

[ALEC *aims at the wall and fires.*]

ROBIN   War isn't exactly a weekend shoot.

ALEC   How would you know? You've never been in uniform.

[ALEC *continues his target practice.*]

ROBIN   Bad eyesight.

HORATIO   [*gleefully*] What did you do on Civvy Street?
            Were you always a reporter?

ROBIN   I was a gigolo. Bad eyesight was an asset.

ALEC   Fantasy.

ROBIN   Don't ask them to send you to the desert.

ALEC   I thought we weren't to discuss this.

HORATIO   Dear boy, they're not going to send *him* to the
            desert. His family is too well connected. Titles
            and everything. They don't kill the posh ones.

ALEC   I'm not planning to be killed. I want to fight.

ROBIN   You're a child.

                    [ROBIN *walks away, onto the balcony.*
                    ALEC *continues shooting at the target.*]

ALEC   He keeps calling me a child. It's very boring. I
            was never a child. Look at my aim. Where *is*
            your rent? This house costs a bloody fortune.

HORATIO   As you said. The dancer.

ALEC   Ah.

HORATIO   She loves me.

ALEC   She should. What do you buy her with my rent
            money? Stockings? Perfume? I hear she's a spy.

HORATIO   For who?

ALEC   The King.

HORATIO   Nonsense.

ALEC   The bloody Nazis, then.

HORATIO   Don't be obscene.

ALEC   She mingles with officers.

HORATIO   So does your Kiwi lover.

ALEC   Perhaps he's a spy.

HORATIO   No, he's from another planet.

ALEC   Too true.

HORATIO   When she leaves the shower . . .

ALEC   Who?

HORATIO   Tahia. The water — clings to her.

ALEC   Doesn't it dry?

HORATIO   It's the way it dries.

ALEC   You're too old for this.

HORATIO   Sometimes — in the shower — her heart sings.

ALEC   What about Emily?

HORATIO   You see me as I was yesterday. I'm not that person any more.

ALEC   Everyone in this house is mad.

> [ALEC *aims away from the wall and shoots a cup on the table. The* DUCHESS *comes in from the hallway, holding her ears.*]

DUCHESS   Boom. Boom. It upsets me.

ALEC   Sorry.

DUCHESS   It is not a toy.

ALEC   I'm not a child.

> [*The* DUCHESS *returns to the hallway. She looks through the pile of luggage and belongings and comes upon a straw hat.* ALEC *returns the pistol to the table drawer.* ROBIN *returns from the balcony and stands watching* ALEC.]

HORATIO   Did *she* pay her rent?

ALEC   The Duchess has credit.

HORATIO   Why?

ALEC   I don't know. I like her.

HORATIO   Where do you find them?

> [*The* DUCHESS *walks back into the sitting room with the straw hat.*]

DUCHESS   May I borrow? For the sun?

ALEC   It's Nigel's.

DUCHESS   But he jumps from an aeroplane over Greece.

ALEC   Parachutes.

DUCHESS   Yes.

ALEC   I suppose he won't be back for a while. Never know who's in this house. Take it. [*looks at the clock*] I have to go. Leave's up.

> [ROBIN *goes to* ALEC *and takes his hand.*]

ROBIN   Don't.

> [ALEC *pulls away.*]

ALEC   Please.

DUCHESS   [*to* HORATIO] Come into the hallway.

HORATIO   Why?

DUCHESS   We will look at Nigel's things.

HORATIO   Why?

> [*The* DUCHESS *nudges him.*]

DUCHESS   Why do you think?

> [HORATIO *and the* DUCHESS *go into the hallway, and search through the belongings, then continue into* NIGEL's *room.*]

ALEC   What are you afraid of?

ROBIN   Darling, I'm never afraid.

ALEC   Don't call me darling in daylight. Why aren't you rustling up a story?

ROBIN   They don't print my stories.

ALEC   Because you're a lazy sod.

ROBIN   You know I have visions.

ALEC   So you say.

ROBIN   I feel things.

ALEC   Yes. Indeed you do.

ROBIN   Don't ask for the desert.

          [ALEC *stares at him.*]

          What are you doing?

ALEC   Nothing much. Just looking at you.

ROBIN   Don't.

ALEC   Why not?

ROBIN   Your eyes are making promises that they're not prepared to keep.

ALEC   That would be dishonest.

ROBIN   Exactly.

ALEC   I've never done anything dishonest in my life.

ROBIN   You have no idea who you are.

ALEC   I know exactly who I am.

ROBIN   Right. You'll be late for your desk.

ALEC   I'm not a desk. I'm a buccaneer. That's who I am. I need adventure. Anyhow, it isn't right for me to enjoy myself while our boys are dying.

ROBIN   Our *boys? You're* a boy.

ALEC   Why do you have to complicate everything? Life
        is fairly simple. The Jerries are bad and we're
        good. I want to be in the desert. I want to kill a
        villain. You're not a Christian, are you? Of
        course not. You have Maori blood. You're a
        pagan and pagans are not easy. Only Chris-
        tians really understand killing. I love your
        pagan body. I'm going to ask for the desert. I
        don't belong behind a desk. You don't under-
        stand me at all. You don't understand God. I
        could eat your pagan body. I have no idea why
        you attract me. You don't belong in my world.
        But there's no need to complicate anything. It's
        all ephemeral anyway. Your newspaper will
        send you someplace else. Sooner or later. If
        they don't fire you for incompetence. When I
        return to England, I'll have to marry. The
        desert is simply an extension of Cairo. It's all a
        mirage. Fever. We don't exist. [*Pause.*] I'll send
        word through Hamid. Later. [*Pause.*] Say some-
        thing. Please.

                    [*A long pause.*]

ROBIN   Well. [*Pause.*] Carmen Miranda reminds me of
        an aboriginal warrior.

ALEC   Just what I was thinking.

ROBIN   May I quote her?

ALEC   I wish you would.

ROBIN   [*sings*] "I, yi, yi, yi, yi,
        I like you very much,
        I, yi, yi, yi, yi,
        I think you're grand."

                    [ROBIN *starts to dance a samba.* ALEC
                    sings and dances with him.]

ROBIN)   "Why, why, why is it that
ALEC)   When I feel your touch . . ."

[ROBIN *and* ALEC *empty the bowl of fruit and place the fruit on their heads, holding it in place as they dance and as they continue to sing the song.* HORATIO *leaves* NIGEL'S *room and walks into the sitting room and watches* ROBIN *and* ALEC *cavort.*]

HORATIO   Suddenly — for the first time — I know we will win the war.

[ALEC *and* ROBIN *stop dancing.* ALEC *looks at* ROBIN, *then moves away.*]

ALEC   Have to go. [*Pause.*] Bye, old chap.

[ALEC *walks hurriedly into the hallway and out the front door.* ROBIN *watches him, then picks up a cup and throws it against the wall, as the* DUCHESS *returns to the sitting room.*]

DUCHESS   What is it?

ROBIN   He's going to die.

DUCHESS   How do you know?

ROBIN   [*smiles*] Ah!

[ROBIN *walks onto the balcony.*]

HORATIO   Play-acting.

DUCHESS   Do you think?

HORATIO   Of course.

DUCHESS   I think — perhaps — passion.

HORATIO   Nonsense. He's in no position to understand passion. It's taken me this long. She loves me! Did I tell you that?

[*Blackout.*]

*The city sounds are drowned out by a jazz band,
playing a mournful Dixieland funeral song.*

The lights rise. Midday.

EMILY — *mid-forties, in a dressing gown — is
sitting at the table, playing with a miniature
female doll, some tape and needles. She is
chanting in Creole. Candles are lit throughout
the room.*

EMILY   [*sings*] "L'Appi vini, le Grand Zombi
           L'Appi vini, pou fe gris-gris."

                    [*The* DUCHESS *enters the sitting room,
                    holding a small package. She watches*
                    EMILY *with some dismay.*]

DUCHESS   What are you singing?

EMILY   A chant.

DUCHESS   Oh. I am not certain about this.

                    [EMILY *goes to the earthenware jar and
                    scoops up some liquid.*]

EMILY   Would you like some goula? [*drinks, makes a
           face*] It's gone off. I'll tart it up later.

DUCHESS   No thank you.

EMILY   Well — just a bit. [*drinks again*] Goes with the
           chanting, I think. [*returns to the table*] A rather
           strange woman, Mazie, what an absurd name,
           married to the Cultural Attaché at the Ameri-
           can Embassy, which must be a totally redun-
           dant position, spent time, Mazie that is, in that
           city with jazz bands and dancing at funerals,
           what's it called, New Orleans, yes of course,
           and she taught me a voodoo chant, evidently
           everyone there practises it, one doesn't usually
           associate Yanks with black magic; well, it's an
           odd old world. Actually it was she, Mazie, who

suggested this doll; oh dear, I can't really catch
my breath. I only have one lung and I talk far
too much for one lung. We both talk too much,
Horatio and I, always have, but then what
existed between us was inordinately based on
talk, but that is something, some kind of bond,
don't you think? — my mind is racing — I
should really leave on the midnight train to
Palestine; if the Germans march in, one has to
be rather strong, I gather; certainly not a
semi-invalid twittering away on a solitary lung;
after all, they will throw people into some kind
of camp, will they not, although diplomats and
their families must have immunity of some
type; I wish Horatio would tell me things; well,
immunity is quite what this little person does
not possess, this Tahia person, this Tahia doll,
this brazen miniature that is about to die.

DUCHESS   I am very nervous. This is not a good thing to
do.

EMILY   I've put a tiny belly dancer's dress on her, not
much of a dress, but a lot of belly; well, as it
should be; do you have to go to belly dancers'
school, do you think, or do you just pick it up?

DUCHESS   I did not realise. I thought at first this was a
joke. Without harm.

EMILY   But you have the package?

DUCHESS   Yes.

EMILY   Hamid gave you the package?

DUCHESS   Yes.

EMILY   And he said it was genuine?

DUCHESS   He said so, yes.

EMILY   And he would not take money?

DUCHESS   No.

EMILY   Interesting.

[*The* DUCHESS *hands the package to* EMILY.]

Thank you. [*opens the package and removes a strand of hair*] A lock of her hair.

DUCHESS   Yes.

EMILY   Tahia's hair.

DUCHESS   Yes.

EMILY   There's henna in it.

DUCHESS   Yes.

EMILY   He said it was genuine?

DUCHESS   Yes.

EMILY   I'll add it to her little wig. [*removes a strand of material*] And this, this . . .

DUCHESS   Fibre.

EMILY   From her costume.

DUCHESS   Yes.

EMILY   I'll attach it to her little dress.

DUCHESS   Air . . .

EMILY   What?

DUCHESS   Air has many things in it. Things we do not understand. We should be careful.

EMILY   Of air? [*laughs*] Oh, Duchess, I am sorry. I am not laughing at you; you have a kind heart, as I once did. I really don't believe you're a Nazi spy.

DUCHESS   What?

EMILY   Oh my dear, everyone says it. But it's just
        tittle-tattle. I would not be sitting here with
        you if I thought it were even remotely true. No,
        I suspect it is rather the opposite and that it is
        you, not I, who should be on that midnight
        train; and well you may be; if Horatio is unable
        to secure you a pass, I just might give you
        mine. I think my place is by my husband's side,
        don't you? And I want to see if the spell works.
        [*drinks from her cup of goula*] It needs sugar.
        [*unfolds a piece of paper*] Mazie said this one
        was highly effective.

        [*She reads from the paper, and sings.*]

"Eh! Eh! Bomba hen hen!
Canga bafie te
Danga moune de te
Cange do ki li
Canga li!"

        [*She throws the paper down.*]

I'm not in good voice. I think you need *two*
lungs for voodoo. I'm ill-prepared for this; in
England most of what we say is mumbo-jumbo,
but it is not literally mumbo-jumbo. Now
Mazie, bless her, told me about a rather
fascinating creature named Marie Laveau, who
was the voodoo queen of New Orleans, it is
utterly amazing the things these American
wives gossip about; well, Marie Laveau reigned
supreme for over one hundred years, which is
quite a trick, and indeed was a trick, for it
seems that after Marie reached middle age, she
retired into her house, and her daughter
emerged and impersonated her mother, so
although she was in fact not really Marie
Laveau neither was she exactly not Marie
Laveau, she was not quite Marie Laveau,

	almost Marie Laveau, if you know what I mean. I suppose if they saw an old woman they would assume she had lost her power.
DUCHESS	I think you are tired. Perhaps if you lie down.
EMILY	He took me to Madame Badia's, you know, the nightclub on the Corniche, on one of my good days. I have good days and bad days, this was in fact a disastrous day disguised as a good one. Everyone was there, at Madame Badia's, princesses and cavalry officers and all the embassy husbands and wives and much of the court including the King, and there was a lot of whisky, and some comedians who told jokes about the Germans, which seemed to please everyone but the King, and then the dancers, who a rather unpleasant Turk called tummy dancers. I found that amusing, and then she came on, the tall version of this doll, and the audience went wild, because her tummy seemed to have danced better than the others, and when she finished, he stood up and went backstage, for a moment, he said, to pay his embassy's respects, as if the British government would have a social contract with a tummy person, and he only a minor official anyhow, and I sat alone, deserted at the table, staring at the whisky and the hummus, and he was absent, backstage, paying respects, for forty minutes, and I sat alone while every fake emir and war profiteer and embassy wife and even the King looked at me, occasionally, in passing, with pity and contempt, and then he returned, his face quite red, and his body obviously with fever, and I said I was humiliated and he said how dare I spoil a lovely evening, a really enchanting night out, and I wished I had had a young daughter who would

at that moment impersonate me, sitting at the table at Madame Badia's, not quite me, but almost. [*Pause.*] All right.

> [EMILY *takes a large pin and raises it in the air, about to strike the doll.*]

Alley-oop!

DUCHESS   Don't! This is not good, this is not good.

EMILY   Oh, Duchess, it is only a doll.

DUCHESS   Please.

EMILY   I'll be gentle.
[*sings*] "L'Appi vini, le Grand Zombi
L'Appi vini, pou fe gris-gris!"

> [EMILY *plunges the needle into the doll's stomach.*]

It's done. [*Pause.*] Poor Tahia. It's not her fault.

> [ROBIN *has entered the hallway from the front door; he walks into the sitting room.*]

ROBIN   Noel Coward is coming to town.

DUCHESS   What?

ROBIN   And possibly Vivien Leigh.

DUCHESS   What do you mean?

> [ROBIN *takes a charred piece of paper from his pocket.*]

ROBIN   A schedule of future concerts, the entire ENSA agenda for the next six months — fell on my head. A bit of it is charred, but even there, if you look very closely, you can make out the name Larry Adler. Of course, this might be a trick, one of your husband's very crafty propaganda coups; sprinkling Cairo with bits of paper promising Larry Adler if everyone resists the Hun. What on earth is going on here?

EMILY   I've just stuck a pin into the belly of a doll.

ROBIN   Whoops.

EMILY   I've become a barbarian. I've surrendered my ba.

ROBIN   Excuse me?

EMILY   In ancient Egypt the inner self was known as the ba. Sometimes the inner self is able to stand at a distance and observe the outer self and it does not always approve of what it sees, oh no, far from it, and sometimes, it is so appalled, it leaves home.

          [ROBIN *stares at her.*]

ROBIN   Oh.

          [*He starts to giggle.*]

EMILY   The pin won't come out. What do I do with the doll now? Mazie never mentioned this part. I want to take the pin out. I'm afraid it's hurting her. I don't want to hurt her.

DUCHESS   It's only a doll.

ROBIN   Who is Mazie?

EMILY   [*screams*] Look at the state I'm in! Look at the state that man has put me into.

ROBIN   What man?

EMILY   [*laughs*] I'm sorry. I'm so sorry. I've just given a mad scene. Oh dear Lord! My mother designed costumes, I grew up around theatres, I know a mad scene when I see one and I just gave one. I've been sticking pins into dolls! I've been chanting in Creole! Discussing my ba! [*holds out the doll*] Dearest Robin, would you do me a major favour, and dispose of this poor thing?

[ROBIN *takes the doll.*]

ROBIN   With pleasure.

[EMILY *rises.*]

EMILY   I think I had better lie down. I'm sorry, Duchess, I don't know what's wrong with me. I'm not usually like this.

> [EMILY *leaves, into the hallway, and then her bedroom.* ROBIN *untacks the photograph of King George from the wall and wraps the doll in it.*]

DUCHESS   The English are very strange. They have much emotion; all the time they have much emotion, and then they say, oh excuse me, I am not usually like this, but they are *always* like this.

> [ROBIN *places the wrapped doll on the table.*]

ROBIN   I'll bury this later. [*blows out the candles*] Everyone in town thinks she's a Nazi spy, Emily. That's why she doesn't leave Horatio. She has to remain close to her source of information. That's what everyone thinks. I'm sure it isn't true.

> [ROBIN *goes to the window and opens the shutters. The sun streams into the room, as does the noise.*]

DUCHESS   No, please, the noise!

ROBIN   I love the noise. And the heat. Even the sand. I'll miss it.

DUCHESS   Miss it?

ROBIN   When I leave. [*goes to the hallway*] Let's read
           Nigel's letters.

DUCHESS   What?

ROBIN   This house is filled with post. Unopened letters.
           And belongings. People drift in and out. Disap-
           pear.

           [*He rummages through a pile and finds a
           group of letters, which he brings with
           him into the sitting room.*]

DUCHESS   It's so hot. It's hard to move. [*looks at the clock*]
           It's midday. I hate to think of outside.

           [ROBIN *spreads the letters on the floor.*]

           Those letters are private.

ROBIN   That's the point.

DUCHESS   I've been already to five embassies this morn-
           ing to arrange a pass. Nothing.

           [ROBIN *opens a letter and starts to read
           it.*]

           He'll be upset.

ROBIN   Who?

DUCHESS   Nigel.

ROBIN   Oh, Nigel's dead.

DUCHESS   How do you know?

ROBIN   [*reading the letter*] Boring. From his Mama.
           About a church service. Flower arrangements.
           The vicar.

DUCHESS   I must try the Canadian Embassy next.

ROBIN   [*opening more letters, reading them*] Brothers
           . . . sisters . . . more church . . . more vicar . . .

no juice . . . not even a blitz . . . with such a
large family, you'd think someone would be in
at least one blitz . . . even a tiny one . . .
Nothing tasty . . . Damn. [*looks up*] I like to
know about other people's lives. [*Pause.*] He
was captured in Greece, actually. The Germans
killed him. Only twenty-six. [*holds up a letter*]
You see — it's a birthday card. I never met
him. I hear he was dishy. [*pushes the letters
aside*] This is depressing. I need music. Sound.

> [ROBIN *rises and goes to the phonograph.
> The* DUCHESS *starts for the hallway.*]

Don't leave. [*Pause.*] Yi deistvitelno gert-
soginya?

DUCHESS   Russian?

ROBIN   Umm. Good guess. Do you know what I said?

DUCHESS   Good Russian — White Russian — families do
not speak Russian. Never did.

ROBIN   I know. [*finds a record, next to the phonograph*]
How about Mozart? Don't leave. What sort of
man do you think Mozart was?

> [*He puts the record on.*]

DUCHESS   It is not of concern to me.

ROBIN   God's problem in life, His only real *raison
d'être*, was to create, wasn't it? And artists
create as well. What's your first language,
Duchess? So are artists part of God?

DUCHESS   You have connections. For your work, you must
know everyone, everyone in town. You have
influence.

ROBIN   I need to hear music before I leave.

DUCHESS   Where do you go?

ROBIN   Do you think Mozart was mortal? Or — better
             still — what about Shakespeare?

DUCHESS   You must be able to secure me a pass. For the
             train. If you wished.

ROBIN   Name me a thought — go ahead — a single
             thought, a feeling — oh, dear, feeling, feeling —
             an emotion — that is not somewhere expressed
             in Shakespeare. How could one man possibly
             know *everything*? Was he human? More than
             human? When you first read Shakespeare,
             Duchess, what language was it in?

DUCHESS   I must take the midnight train to Palestine.

ROBIN   Of course you must. You're Jewish.

DUCHESS   No.

ROBIN   Every Jew in Cairo is trying to leave.

DUCHESS   No. I simple like to be two steps ahead . . .

ROBIN   Of . . .

DUCHESS   The Germans.

ROBIN   Shakespeare and Mozart were probably gods, if
             a god means not entirely human. Or were they?

DUCHESS   Yes — yes — Of course I'm Jewish.

ROBIN   Not a Duchess?

DUCHESS   Oh don't be so stupid! Do I look like a duchess?
             No one in Cairo believes I am a duchess.

ROBIN   Just listen to the music . . .

DUCHESS   You are a reporter. You need stories. I will give
             you my story. In return for a pass for the
             midnight train to Palestine.

ROBIN   I know your story.

DUCHESS   How can you?

ROBIN   I see you every day. You and yours. Now, my immediate guess would be Polish. Are you Polish? Yes, I'd wager that. Not Russian certainly. A good family, I would think. A fine education. Languages. But the Gestapo doesn't care about breeding. Wouldn't know it, actually, would it? Would only know you were a Jew. So where did your family end up? A ghetto? I would think. Did you escape? Was that the start of many adventures? You were clever, you had imagination, you went for a grand deception, you masqueraded as royalty, because no one knows who is or isn't or was or wasn't any more, and anyhow the more outrageous the lie the better your chances. Am I accurate?

DUCHESS   More or less.

ROBIN   It's an old story, Duchess, and my readers don't care about it. They don't want to know. It's not their life. It's not their world. It's not familiar enough. Listen to the music . . .

DUCHESS   But it's only part of the story.

ROBIN   Oh?

DUCHESS   I did not escape alone. I left with my lover.

ROBIN   Yes?

DUCHESS   My cousin.

ROBIN   Yes?

DUCHESS   Sophia.

ROBIN   [*smiles*] Yes, of course.

DUCHESS   Our family did not exactly approve. Ach, to be so blind, so blind. If we had had their blessing! Well. We escaped the ghetto and the Gestapo *and* the family. Sophia was — is — my life. But she was — what? — careless. She made a mistake. She was captured. They murdered her. Christians murdered her, people who believe in that God who creates. She was my life.

ROBIN   I'm sorry.

DUCHESS   Listen to your music. I do not hear music any more. I do not wish to live without the taste of Sophia. But I am compelled to live. It is a nasty habit, this living, a narcotic, bad for you, but you cannot give it up. Sophia is inside of me. I do not want them to kill her twice. I must have a pass for the midnight train to Palestine.

ROBIN   Perhaps you will find her in another life.

DUCHESS   Yes. A nice thought.

ROBIN   I'm quite serious.

DUCHESS   Oh.

ROBIN   Do you not believe in other lives?

DUCHESS   To think of childhood again, adolescence again, family again, Gestapos again, again many times; no, I am too tired to be reborn. And then not to remember this life. Not to remember Sophia. No.

ROBIN   But to meet Sophia. Again.

DUCHESS   I think you are perhaps mad.

ROBIN   I don't like to do this. Because it hurts me.

DUCHESS   Do what?

ROBIN   This.

            [*He puts his palms against his forehead, and presses tightly. He winces.*]

DUCHESS   What is this?

ROBIN	Concentration. Little electric shocks whizz through my head. I hate it.
DUCHESS	What are you talking about?
ROBIN	But it's the only way.
DUCHESS	To do what?
ROBIN	See the future. Bits of it.

[*He presses his palms harder. He is breathing faster and gasping for air.*]

DUCHESS	No . . . Stop . . .
ROBIN	I can tell you about Sophia.
DUCHESS	You are making fun of me.
ROBIN	I am helping you. Ouch! It hurts! It stings! I hate this! She is already back.
DUCHESS	This is not right . . .
ROBIN	Back here.
DUCHESS	Where?
ROBIN	On earth. where do you think? Aren't you listening? She is back on earth. In another form, of course. Watching over you.
DUCHESS	How dare you do this to me . . .
ROBIN	And then . . . Ouch! Damn it! Shit! And then . . . yes, I can see it . . . Bits of it . . .
DUCHESS	You're making this into a joke . . .
ROBIN	Many lives from now — quite a few, a bit of a wait, I'm afraid, but still — you are united, you and Sophia, in an unusual and very beautiful way . . .
DUCHESS	Stop!

ROBIN   Oh yes . . . Ouch! Fuck! Damn! It's what you
           have been moving toward . . .

DUCHESS   Stop!

ROBIN   It is finally — finally — many lives from now . . .
           something good . . .

DUCHESS   Stop! It wasn't true! It was a lie.

ROBIN   You will be together . . .

DUCHESS   There was no Sophia! It was a lie! Stop —
           please! I am not even a Jew. I made it up. I
           made it up to interest you. I wanted a pass for
           the train.

ROBIN   Trust me. Look into my eyes.

DUCHESS   No.

ROBIN   Into my eyes . . .

DUCHESS   I'm afraid.

ROBIN   My eyes . . .

DUCHESS   Don't do this to me. Please. I cannot even
           believe in what I see today. I only want to be
           two steps ahead. Only two. Don't do this to me.

           [*The hands on the grandfather clock
           suddenly start to rotate at a furious pace,
           and the clock starts to chime.*]

ROBIN   Damn!

DUCHESS   What is it?

ROBIN   Time has gone haywire. How's your watch?

           [*The* DUCHESS *looks at her watch.*]

DUCHESS   Stopped.

ROBIN   It's so annoying.

DUCHESS   Those chimes . . .

ROBIN   Did the spoons bend?

DUCHESS   What?

ROBIN   Look at the spoons.

DUCHESS   What spoons?

ROBIN   On the table.

> [*The* DUCHESS *goes to the table, opens a drawer, and removes some silver. The clock continues to chime, and its hands revolve.*]

DUCHESS   Oh. Yes. [*examining spoons*] They are crooked.

ROBIN   That happens. Damn. And now I have a splitting headache.

DUCHESS   Forks as well. All the silver.

ROBIN   Nothing is simple. Why isn't anything simple?

> [*He carries a chair over to the clock.*]

DUCHESS   You've made me shake.

> [ROBIN *stands on the chair and begins to fiddle with the hands of the clock.*]

ROBIN   All right! All right! [*to the clock*] I hear you.

DUCHESS   Not even the thought of Gestapo does that. I promise myself I will never shake again.

ROBIN   Sorry, Duchess.

DUCHESS   I cannot absorb . . .

ROBIN   Don't try. [*to the clock*] All right!

DUCHESS   I think perhaps I go to Canadian Embassy.

> [*The* DUCHESS *quietly walks into the hallway and out the front door.* ROBIN *does not see her leave.*]

ROBIN   No, don't. Don't leave. This racket will stop in a
             minute, I promise. The energy just runs ber-
             serk, that's all. Look, Duchess, I haven't been
             entirely honest with you. There is something I
             probably should tell you. I'm afraid you will
             laugh at me. Well, it goes without saying — you
             will laugh. It always happens, the few times
             I've ever attempted this kind of truth. Nervous
             laughter. There! Back to normal.

                      [*The chimes stop. The hands of the clock
                      are back in their proper place.* ROBIN *sits
                      on the chair, still unaware of the* DUCH-
                      ESS's *absence.*]

             But I really should tell you. I did see Sophia. In
             this life. In this incarnation. She's . . . oh dear,
             you will laugh, you will . . . Thank God I can't
             see your face. She's . . . oh, this is ridiculous, I
             can't say this, you think me crazy already, don't
             you? Don't answer that. Well, I suppose I
             should give it a whack, it's only fair, you should
             know. She's . . . oh, no, I can't, I really can't —
             well, I'll close my eyes, that will make it easier
             — all right? She's . . . here goes, one, two, three
             . . . She's a cockroach. Actually. I'm afraid.
             She's come back as a cockroach. Well, we can't
             all be pharaohs or presidents each time, it's not
             always Cleopatra and it's not always a horse;
             but perhaps she's only in as a cockroach for a
             short stay, I don't know, the picture became
             blurred. Are you laughing? I can hardly blame
             you; I found myself giggling when Emily talked
             about her ba — it is, after all, a funny word —
             all I could think of was baa baa black sheep —
             but the irony is I believe in it, in inner life,
             outer life, everything she said. But I did laugh.
             I suppose I might as well go all the way now. I
             suppose I might as well tell you the complete

truth. I've wanted to tell someone all day; I've had an uncontrollable urge. Even though my instructions are very precise — say nothing, confide in no one. But you see, I did not expect feelings. Feelings. I've only known Alec for two weeks and he is a bit of an upper-class twit, I know that, but who can possibly explain these things, these bizarre human emotions, very odd — feelings are foreign matter in my system and everything is the opposite of what it should be and I am on very dangerous ground because I want to tell the truth even though I promised not to; I'm going to have to look into your eyes if I break my promise, Duchess, I'm . . .

> [*He turns around.* HAMID *has entered the house and stands in the doorway.*]

Duchess?

HAMID   Only Hamid.

ROBIN   Oh. [*Pause.*] I was talking to myself.

HAMID   Yes. British always talk to empty rooms.

ROBIN   I'm not British.

HAMID   I have package for Mrs Walker.

ROBIN   I'll take it.

> [HAMID *hands* ROBIN *a small package.*]

HAMID   Eyelash.

ROBIN   The belly dancer's?

HAMID   Indeed.

ROBIN   It won't be needed now.

HAMID   And this. [*removes a piece of charred paper from his pocket*] Fall on my head. Words in code.

ROBIN   Oh. Let me see.

[HAMID *hands the paper to* ROBIN.]

HAMID   Important?

ROBIN   [*examining the paper*] Can't tell . . .

HAMID   Worth money?

ROBIN   It's quite burnt. Ah . . . [*finds a portion that is reasonably intact*] "We'll meet again, Don't know where, Don't know when . . . " [*laughs*] Bad luck, Hamid. Look, I'd rather like to go to the Pyramids.

HAMID   Many soldiers there.

ROBIN   You can get me through.

HAMID   Indeed.

ROBIN   I would not mind one last look.

HAMID   [*points to the paper*] Worth nothing?

ROBIN   [*reads*] "But I know we'll meet again some sunny day." [*crumples the paper up*] Nothing.

          [*Blackout.*]

A mélange of Mozart, Vera Lynn, Dixieland and street cries.

The lights rise. Late afternoon.

EMILY *is on the floor with a duster and rag, cleaning and putting the room in order.*

HORATIO *enters.* EMILY *does not look up.*

HORATIO   What are you doing?

EMILY   What does it look like I'm doing?

HORATIO   Cleaning, I'd say.

EMILY Aha!

HORATIO Why are you cleaning?

EMILY Why?

HORATIO That's what I asked.

EMILY Why?

HORATIO Yes, why.

EMILY Because the house is a right old mess. Or haven't you noticed?

HORATIO Where is Aziz?

EMILY Where is Aziz?

HORATIO That's what I asked.

EMILY I know. I'm repeating it.

HORATIO Why are you repeating it?

EMILY Because I can't believe you asked.

HORATIO Well, I did ask. It's a reasonable question. Where is Aziz?

EMILY Where is Aziz indeed?

HORATIO Indeed. Where is he?

EMILY Who?

HORATIO Aziz, damn it.

EMILY Don't know, do I?

[HORATIO *goes into the hallway and sifts through the luggage. He calls out to* EMILY.]

HORATIO The servants should clean.

EMILY The servants, including Aziz, have not been here for two days, my dear. Or haven't you noticed? Been preoccupied, haven't we?

HORATIO   Why haven't they been here?

EMILY   Worried about the Germans.

HORATIO   So?

EMILY   In case they enter town.

HORATIO   Yes?

EMILY   They don't want to be caught working for the Brits.

HORATIO   Bloody nonsense.

EMILY   Is it?

HORATIO   The Jerries will never take Cairo.

> [HORATIO *brings two pieces of luggage into the sitting room. He sits on the floor and opens them.*]

EMILY   Save the party line for the fortune-tellers.

HORATIO   Well, yes, all right, I concede — slightly. Anything is possible. Rommel is meant to be a very clever chap. Brave as well. Leads his men into battle himself. To tell you the truth, I don't really care. The war is simply background noise.

EMILY   What's in the foreground?

HORATIO   My heart, actually.

EMILY   Do you know what upsets me — what really upsets me — is that I typed phrases like that in your manuscripts time and time again and I never laughed.

HORATIO   You have become unpleasant.

EMILY   I'm no longer colourless. I've been colourless for years. Thank you for that, I suppose.

> [HORATIO *is carefully sifting through the contents of the luggage.*]

EMILY   What on earth are you doing?

HORATIO   Searching.

EMILY   Those are Nigel's belongings.

HORATIO   I am aware of that.

EMILY   His letters are scattered on the floor. Did you do that?

HORAATIO   Of course not. I don't read other people's post.

EMILY   How can I clean if you make more of a mess?

HORATIO   Stop cleaning. Sit down.

EMILY   What exactly are you doing?

HORATIO   As I said — searching.

EMILY   Without Nigel's permission?

HORATIO   [*removes a charred piece of paper from his pocket*] This fell on my head. It's a list of recent casualties in Greece. Nigel's name is on the list — at least it appears to be Nigel's name. A few letters have turned to ash.

EMILY   Oh.

HORATIO   The list hasn't been released by the War Office so it's top secret.

EMILY   Obviously.

HORATIO   I do wish the chaps at the embassy would burn these things thoroughly or at least wait until there's no wind. Still, it might be a brilliant tactic. The Germans will be unable to discover any secrets if nothing remains secret.

EMILY   I thought we weren't to worry about the Germans.

HORATIO   We're not to. It's just a precaution. At any rate, old Nigel has bought it.

EMILY   Poor Nigel.

HORATIO   Really, you can stop cleaning now. The dust is
           bad for your lung.

EMILY   I know. I might die.

HORATIO   You might indeed. Damn, where on earth is it?

EMILY   Where is what?

HORATIO   What I'm searching for.

EMILY   Death by dust.

HORATIO   What?

EMILY   I'd suffer death by dust. Very Egyptian. Dust to
           dust.

HORATIO   Look, put that rag away, and sit down. You're
           making me nervous.

           [*He reaches for the rag and grabs* EMILY
           by her shoulders.]

EMILY   Keep your hands off me.

HORATIO   Emily . . .

EMILY   Your hands smell of oil and perfume.

HORATIO   Emily . . .

EMILY   All the perfumes of Arabia.

HORATIO   All the what?

EMILY   Perfumes of Arabia. [*Pause.*] Oh God. Oh dear
           God. [*Pause.*] Did I say that?

HORATIO   I'm afraid you did.

EMILY   I've done it again. I've given another mad
           scene. I've been doing it all day. But this time
           I've gone too far. I've given someone else's mad
           scene. [*rises*] I would like to behave better.

[HORATIO *finds a package in the luggage. It is tied tightly with string.*]

HORATIO   Ah. This might be it. I need a knife.

EMILY   What?

HORATIO   Find me a knife.

EMILY   I thought you wanted me to sit.

HORATIO   Well, yes, in due time.

EMILY   The servants will find you a knife.

HORATIO   The servants are not here.

EMILY   Oh. Really. [*walks to the table*] That was our marriage, wasn't it?

HORATIO   What was?

EMILY   "Sit down. No — wait. Get me something. Hurry." Marriage. [*takes out the silver and examines the knives*] I'm afraid they're all bent.

HORATIO   What?

EMILY   The knives are bent. That's odd.

HORATIO   Don't be ridiculous.

EMILY   And the forks and spoons. I think I should tell you something. I put a curse on Fatima this morning.

HORATIO   Who is Fatima?

EMILY   You know, what's-her-name — Tahia.

HORATIO   I don't wish to discuss it. There must be a usable knife there.

EMILY   [*picks up a knife*] Well, this one is almost straight.

[*She hands it to* HORATIO.]

HORATIO   Thank you.

EMILY   I made a voodoo doll. I even sang a little voodoo song. It was completely childish of me. I feel terribly guilty about it.

            [HORATIO *has cut the string with the knife. He opens the package and removes a pearl necklace.*]

HORATIO   There.

EMILY   What on earth?

HORATIO   [*holds the necklace up to the light*] Absolutely beautiful.

EMILY   Yes.

HORATIO   Nigel purchased this for his mother.

EMILY   And you're going to send it to her.

HORATIO   Don't be daft.

EMILY   You're not . . .

HORATIO   Spoils of war.

EMILY   You're stealing a dead man's property?

HORATIO   That's an ugly way of putting it. This will never — never — reach his mother. The War Office is obviously going to wait a long time until they admit he's dead. By then Alec will have given up this house — might be dead himself, our Alec, you never know — and all these belongings will have found their way to the black market or, if the Jerries do happen to come in, will be confiscated by some Nazi beast. I am, in my way, honouring Nigel's memory, and the cause he gave his life for; certainly he would prefer a friend to have this.

EMILY   You hardly knew him.

HORATIO   Hardly's a lot in wartime. Don't you dare try to make me feel guilty.

EMILY   Oh. Of course. I see.

HORATIO   See what?

EMILY   It's for her.

HORATIO   Ah. For Fatima?

EMILY   Tahia.

HORATIO   As a matter of fact . . .

EMILY   How can you be so . . . ?

HORATIO   So what? You people utterly fail to understand.

EMILY   Pardon me, who exactly are you people?

HORATIO   Everyone else. None of you understand. I always felt inadequate, that's the truth, a very painful truth, although it probably never occurred to you. Now suddenly, for the first time, I am the centre of my universe, and I am saddened to discover not a single planet revolving around me. Well, not any of the old planets, the planets I used to know and trust. I've happened onto a new solar system, you might say. Look, I am not young; I am past fifty, and the rocks are about to slide down the mountain. Do you understand? It's as if all the gifts I was ever given were on loan, and they all now slowly have to be returned. I thought I had purchased a house, but now I realise I'm only renting. And when it's all over, I will have learnt nothing. Not unlike civilization; centuries and centuries, and we have learnt nothing. Do you understand? And then suddenly — magically — this creature appeared, from nowhere, from Madame Badia's palace of pleasure, and this creature did a remarkable thing. She loved me. And now I feel as if I'm dreaming, or I feel as if I'm awake, one or the other, I don't know which, both perhaps at the same time. She has transmuted me into another world.

EMILY   I feel really ill.

HORATIO   She writes poems about me. Did I tell you that? It should embarrass me, I know, but it fills me with wonder.

EMILY   I don't want to hear this.

HORATIO   Poems of such delicacy . . .

EMILY   What rhymes with Horatio?

HORATIO   And beauty . . .

EMILY   Does she write in English?

HORATIO   Arabic.

EMILY   You don't read Arabic.

HORATIO   I understand the gist. Love is about gist.

EMILY   I don't think you can hear yourself. You've become an adolescent.

HORATIO   I want you to accept what's happened.

EMILY   An adolescent grave robber.

HORATIO   I want you to be happy for me.

EMILY   I'm truly ill.

HORATIO   If you loved me, you'd be happy for me.

EMILY   My head is pounding.

HORATIO   You'd rejoice for me.

EMILY   Are you mad?

HORATIO   How long will you continue to persecute me like this?

EMILY   What?

HORATIO   How long will you continue to make me suffer?

EMILY   I think I've lost the plot.

HORATIO   How can you treat me so badly?

EMILY   Treat you badly! My dear, I have been a faithful and yes, as I suggested, a colourless wife for twenty years, colourless because you drained the reds and greens and yellows from me, which I allowed, because you absorbed them and took sustenance from them, and became, in your way — using my colours — a rainbow. Perhaps if we had had children we might have been obsessed with something other than ourselves; we were our own children, which is hardly uncommon, and I suppose our own posterity. And Emily and Horatio, though a rather unwieldy phrase, became one word. I suppose I've asked for very little, and perhaps that's a crime, but I do not deserve this humiliation.

HORATIO   You're talking about yesterday. But it's not yesterday. It's tomorrow.

EMILY   Actually, it's today.

HORATIO   I want you to meet her.

EMILY   What?

HORATIO   I want to bring her to this house.

EMILY   I'm hallucinating.

HORATIO   In fact, we, both of us, together, might give her the necklace.

EMILY   I'm hurtling through space.

HORATIO   I think you will like her. When you see how much she loves me, you will like her. And when you like her, you will be happy. Really — that is what I want — your happiness. I want you to be happy for me.

[EMILY *stares at him. A pause.*]

EMILY   Train.

HORATIO   What?

EMILY   I must take the train.

HORATIO   What train?

EMILY   At midnight.

HORATIO   Where to?

EMILY   Palestine.

HORATIO   Nonsense.

EMILY   I have to leave Cairo. You're mad. Or I'm mad. Someone's mad. Do you have my ticket?

HORATIO   Your what?

EMILY   Ticket. My pass.

HORATIO   No. Of course not.

EMILY   What do you mean, no?

HORATIO   I mean N–O. No.

EMILY   Why not?

HORATIO   I want you by my side. You're my wife. And I want you to meet Tahia. I want you to see us together. I want you to be happy for me.

EMILY   You are mad.

HORATIO   You're my wife.

EMILY   You will probably hand me over to the Germans when they arrive.

HORATIO   They are not going to arrive.

EMILY   What does that American comedian on the radio say — "Take my wife"? That's what you'll say to the Nazis. You probably have an arrangement with them. *You* are probably the spy everyone is whispering about. This is a subtle way of killing me. You'll hand me over. You will strip me of diplomatic immunity. One lung in a dirty prison camp. Talk about dust. I'll be dead within hours.

HORATIO   You are really beginning to upset me . . .

EMILY   You want me to die.

HORATIO   You mustn't say that.

EMILY   You want me dead.

HORATIO   Why am I somehow always in the wrong?

EMILY   You want me dead.

HORATIO   You must not say that!

EMILY   You want me dead.

HORATIO   I want you to be quiet.

EMILY   Dead *is* quiet. Totally quiet. You want me dead.

HORATIO   Don't make me hate you.

EMILY   Dead.

HORATIO   It's not true.

EMILY   Dead.

HORATIO   Stop it.

EMILY   Dead.

HORATIO   STOP!

[HORATIO *takes the knife and plunges it into* EMILY's *stomach.* EMILY *holds onto his shoulder, her eyes wide open.*]

HORATIO   Oh, my dear, it was only another mad scene.

> [EMILY *slips to the floor, dead.* HORATIO *stands over her, holding the knife.*]

Look what you've made me do.

> [ROBIN *has entered the hallway from the front door. He walks into the sitting room. He surveys the scene.*]

ROBIN   Well, well, well.

End of Act One

ACT TWO

Early evening.

The room has been tidied up. EMILY's *body has been removed. A piano is heard playing in one of the rooms off the hallway. Mozart.*

The DUCHESS *sits in a chair, her eyes closed, listening to the music.*

HAMID *enters. The* DUCHESS *looks up.*

DUCHESS   Oh! I am sorry. I was someplace else. It is the Mozart.

HAMID   Yes?

DUCHESS   Yes. Did you find him?

HAMID   No.

DUCHESS   But you looked?

HAMID   Yes. I look.

DUCHESS   Where?

HAMID   At Shepherds. I speak to Ali, the porter. Mr Robin is not there. At Anglo-Egyptian Club. I speak to Rashid, the porter. Mr Robin is not there.

DUCHESS   But you saw him in the afternoon?

HAMID   Yes. Indeed. I take him to Pyramids. He wish to climb pyramid.

DUCHESS   Did he?

HAMID   Big one. Yes. Indeed. He climb big pyramid. And he sing.

DUCHESS   Sing?

HAMID   Make noises. Like worship.

DUCHESS   Strange.

HAMID   No. It is strange to just look at pyramid, just look and be silent.

DUCHESS   And that was the last time you saw him?

HAMID   [*turns and heads for hallway*] I look for him again.

> [HAMID *leaves the house. The* DUCHESS *sits down again and listens to the music.* HORATIO *enters from the front door. He walks into the sitting room.*]

HORATIO   Who's playing the bloody piano?

DUCHESS   Alec.

HORATIO   I didn't know he had a piano.

DUCHESS   In his bedroom.

HORATIO   That's a ridiculous place for a piano.

DUCHESS   He does not like people to watch him when he plays.

HORATIO   This house is filled with lunatics.

> [HORATIO *walks back into the hallway and into his bedroom. The piano stops.* ALEC *comes out from his bedroom, through the hallway, to the sitting room.*]

ALEC   Robin?

DUCHESS   Horatio.

ALEC   Damn.

DUCHESS   I sent Hamid to look for him.

ALEC   I only have a few minutes.

DUCHESS   It was very beautiful.

ALEC   What was?

DUCHESS   The Mozart.

ALEC   Oh yes. Do you think? It soothes my nerves, actually. I've been told I have a gift, but I'm — uh, what's a good word?

DUCHESS   Lazy.

ALEC   That's a good word. Indolent. That's better. [*Pause.*] Rich. That's best.

DUCHESS   [*laughs*] I suppose.

ALEC   To tell you the truth, rich doesn't bother me. It's actually quite pleasant. But to be born with a gift — now, that's upsetting. I didn't ask for it, I don't know what to do with it, others would kill for it. It makes no sense. Damn. Double damn. I really must see him. Where do you think he is? You don't imagine he has suddenly decided to file a story, do you? Or even worse — *look* for a story? Gosh. Perhaps he's at the station. I hear there were riots. People trying to leave the city. Triple damn. Times four.

DUCHESS   The station. Yes. [*rises*] I must go once again to the station.

ALEC   Why?

DUCHESS   Why? Because that is where the trains are.

ALEC   Oh.

DUCHESS   Perhaps I meet someone I know, someone I have lied to very well, someone who will find me a pass for the midnight train.

ALEC   I wish I was able to help, Duchess.

DUCHESS   I know.

ALEC   I did ask.

DUCHESS   I know you did. I will search for Robin at the station.

[*She kisses* ALEC *on the forehead.*]

Sweet. [*walks to hallway*] Perhaps you should listen to him.

ALEC   Who?

DUCHESS   Robin.

ALEC   About what?

DUCHESS   About the desert.

ALEC   [*smiles*] Too late.

DUCHESS   Ah.

[*The* DUCHESS *leaves the house.* ALEC *walks to the window and looks outside. He closes the shutters. The room is dark. He turns the light switch on.* HORATIO *is standing in the doorway.* ALEC *winces.*]

ALEC   You gave me a scare.

HORATIO   If only . . .

ALEC   If only what?

HORATIO   If only that were true. If only I were able to frighten someone. Make my presence felt. Ah, well, I think I'm melancholy.

ALEC   I must return. [*Pause.*] I've received my orders. [*Pause.*] I hoped to see Robin before I left. We're unable to find him. [*Pause.*] I'm suddenly nervous. I was desperate for the desert, but I already miss my desk. Nothing happens at a desk. You can get hurt in a desert.

HORATIO   It's an almost tender sadness, this.

ALEC   What?

HORATIO   This melancholy.

ALEC   Look, have you encountered Robin at all this afternoon?

HORATIO   Why do you ask?

ALEC   I'm trying to find him.

HORATIO   Do you think I've seen him?

ALEC   That's what I'm asking.

HORATIO   What are you hinting at?

ALEC   I simply want to know if you've run into him.

HORATIO   Haven't now, have I?

ALEC   Have you?

HORATIO   Not since this morning.

ALEC   I have to go. [*Pause.*] Would you give him a message?

HORATIO   Who?

ALEC   Robin. When you do see him.

HORATIO   Why do you suppose I will see him?

ALEC   You live in the same house.

HORATIO   What are you insinuating?

ALEC   Surely you will see him at some time. What's wrong with you?

HORATIO   Why do you think something is wrong?

ALEC   I can't bear this. I have to go. But I must leave him a message. Damn. Horatio — please!

HORATIO   Well. [*Pause.*] I'm moved too easily. That's really my problem. I have no mind of my own. [*Pause.*] What exactly do you wish me to tell him?

ALEC   They've spoken to me about him. At Headquar-
          ters. They've heard stories about our relation-
          ship.

HORATIO   Oh dear.

ALEC   Well, I don't think they really believe an officer
          might be queer, so *that* isn't an issue — yet.
          They have it down to an undesirable friendship.
          The thing is — they think Robin might be a
          spy.

HORATIO   A spy?

ALEC   Yes, for the Germans.

HORATIO   I see.

ALEC   Something about his papers. Not quite legiti-
          mate. And someone in the newsroom in Auck-
          land claims not to have heard of him. They
          won't tell me details. They're keeping an eye on
          him.

HORATIO   Keeping an eye on him?

ALEC   Yes.

HORATIO   Following his every move?

ALEC   I don't know. Perhaps.

HORATIO   I see.

ALEC   I want you to warn him. It's ridiculous, I'm
          certain he's not a spy. He's a bit flaky, and
          rather elusive, but if those were spy qualifica-
          tions, I'd be a contender as well.

HORATIO   Indeed.

ALEC   Yes. Well. What a thought. [*amused*] Don't
          dismiss it. [*Pause.*] Look, I'm perfectly aware
          that it's not quite cricket to alert him, but then
          cricket doesn't enter into it. I have so many
          conflicting feelings, and some of them are

downright, I don't know what the word is, oh yes I do, downright obsessive, that's it. Do you understand how I feel?

[*Pause.*]

HORATIO   No.

ALEC   Oh. I don't either. I dream about him. My dreams are normally filled with strangers. But now a real person is running through them, causing havoc. Where do dreams come from? Damn. I'm not even sure if I like him. And I'm certainly not sure that I know who he really is. He used to be a gigolo. Did he tell you that? It probably isn't true. Please — warn him.

HORATIO   All right.

ALEC   I want you to give your word.

HORATIO   I did. I said all right.

ALEC   Say "I give you my word".

HORATIO   Don't be an idiot.

ALEC   Say it out loud — please.

HORATIO   Oh dear. I'm so pliable. It infuriates me. [*sighs*] I give you my word. Will that do?

ALEC   Of honour?

HORATIO   Yes. Yes.

ALEC   But will you keep your word? Oh, it's all nonsense, anyway. I won't see him again, no matter what. We're all in transit, aren't we? I must go. Thank you, Horatio. Best to Emily.

HORATIO   What do you mean?

ALEC   Send regards to Emily.

HORATIO   What are you attempting to say?

ALEC   What I said. That's all. My regards to your
            wife.

HORATIO   What are you trying to suggest?

ALEC   Nothing.

HORATIO   If you suspect something, say it.

ALEC   Look, I *must* go. I'm completely late. Just tell
            Robin . . . no, don't tell him anything. Simply
            warn him. I have your word, don't I? Tell him
            . . . no . . . no . . . only what we discussed.
            That's all. Damn. Nothing makes sense, does
            it? I must go.

HORATIO   Goodbye, then.

ALEC   Yes.

            [ALEC *hesitates, then leaves.* HORATIO *im-
            mediately goes to the centre of the room
            and examines the floor, looking for blood-
            stains.* ROBIN *enters from behind the
            screen. He wears a flowing white Bedouin
            robe and a hood.*]

ROBIN   Nothing's there.

HORATIO   Good Lord!

ROBIN   As I promised, not a trace.

HORATIO   What are you dressed as?

            [ROBIN *removes his hood, and paces
            round the room.*]

ROBIN   T.E. Lawrence, I think. Well, I was aiming for
            T.E. Do you think it looks a bit more like
            Gertrude Lawrence? Split the difference. I
            needed a disguise. Some blokes were following
            me. No harm in it, I suppose, but I don't care
            for the feeling. [*holds up a package*] I bought a
            recording in the souk. Something the Yanks are

fond of. I am as well. I wanted to hear it before I left. [*puts the package next to the phonograph*] It's wonderful wearing this. It makes you feel so local. I went for a long walk. Lots of alleyways, courtyards. I was lost. I was on a street filled with coloured booths. Women sitting in coloured booths. They were prostitutes. Each booth had a drawing of a palm, with its fingers outstretched. That's to ward off the evil eye. Then I felt something under my robe, something tugging at my leg, a hand moving up my thigh, and I kicked, and a child scampered out, out from under my robe, it was like a circus act, I don't know how she got there, then she started talking, little, little sentences, she asked me to go with her . . .

HORATIO   How do you know?

ROBIN   Oh, I speak the language. Any dialect.

HORATIO   Do you?

ROBIN   And then I realised I was standing in front of a child brothel, little girls and little boys in coloured booths, protected by the magic palm, and when I say child, none of them older than nine or ten, and it's not that it was shocking or indecent, of course it was, but far more than that, it was impossible to understand — how did they get there, were they stolen, had they been sold, what were their lives like, did the magic palm really protect them, and who would walk into the booth, what kind of person would walk into the coloured booth, and then of course at that moment I was desperate to walk into the coloured booth myself, just to see, just to discover, just to understand something that was beyond understanding. But there was no time. It's over. Cairo is over. And I've learnt so little. [*Pause.*] It wasn't easy finding my way home. It was a labyrinth. I thought I knew the city. Why didn't I dress like this before? [*Pause.*] As soon as I found our street, I knew he was here. I saw him through the window. I climbed up our balcony. I wanted to be near him. But not to see him. Not to speak to him. Not to say goodbye again. They never told me this would happen. I couldn't make out the conversation. What was he saying?

HORATIO   Nothing much.

ROBIN   Did he mention me?

HORATIO   Not really.

ROBIN   Has he forgotten me? Oh, that's ridiculous. I wanted to touch him. [*Pause.*] He's going to the desert, of course.

HORATIO   You said you were followed.

ROBIN   Did I?

HORATIO   But that must mean . . .

ROBIN   Nothing. Hamid took care of the body, not me. Is that what you were worried about? There's no problem.

HORATIO   But then Hamid . . .

ROBIN   Knows no details. Did not ask. Never will. He was handsomely rewarded. She will never be discovered.

HORATIO   It's better, you know. This way. She was ill, after all. Only one lung, and that one ailing. She would have died. It would have been painful and degrading. I think like most people she was afraid of dying rather than death. I've spared her.

ROBIN   What a fine person you are.

HORATIO I'm trying to explain . . .

ROBIN Don't. [*Pause.*] Are you certain he didn't mention me? He had to. I wanted to see him but it was pointless. There wasn't anything I could say to stop him. I feel so strange. I'm mortified. I want to say things about myself that are so inane they must have been written by you. [*Pause.*] I have a pain in my heart. There — I said it. Is it in one of your novels?

HORATIO I don't think so.

ROBIN Then you have my permission to use it. It's true, damn it, though, it's true!

HORATIO Are you positive they didn't see him?

ROBIN Who?

HORATIO Hamid.

ROBIN Who's they?

HORATIO Anyone. Anyone.

ROBIN Don't be concerned.

HORATIO He had a dead body with him.

ROBIN Please! It's Cairo. [*Pause.*] All right — I've fulfilled my end of the bargain.

HORATIO Yes.

ROBIN Your turn now.

HORATIO It's difficult.

ROBIN I don't care.

HORATIO I will meet enormous resistance.

ROBIN You might have thought of that earlier. You made a promise.

HORATIO I was in a panic.

ROBIN	You made a promise.
HORATIO	I was feverish.
ROBIN	You promised you would obtain a pass for the Duchess. From the Embassy.
HORATIO	I had no idea what I was saying.
ROBIN	A pass for the midnight train.
HORATIO	They think she's a gun-runner.
ROBIN	A what?
HORATIO	A gun-runner for the Jewish Underground, the Irgun.
ROBIN	The *Duchess*?
HORATIO	The Embassy has long suspected her. She's on a list.
ROBIN	A list?
HORATIO	Yes.
ROBIN	They've burned their lists. Which means it's probably floating onto someone's head at this very moment.
HORATIO	They think she is planning assassinations.
ROBIN	Mozel-tov. Good for her. Look, it is fiendishly simple. You either find a pass for the Duchess or Emily's body will be discovered. Along with the knife. And your fingerprints.
HORATIO	That's blackmail. That's immoral!
ROBIN	[*laughs*] I'm so sorry to disturb your ethical code. Listen, darling, I want the pass.
HORATIO	Don't call me darling.
ROBIN	The Duchess is going to Palestine.
HORATIO	Why does that matter to you?

ROBIN   I don't know. [*Pause.*] Are you off to the Embassy or do I find Hamid?

            [HORATIO *walks to the hallway. He hesitates.*]

HORATIO   It isn't easy for me, you know.

ROBIN   Oh?

HORATIO   You see, I can't imagine a life without her.

ROBIN   The dancer?

HORATIO   No. Emily.

            [HORATIO *leaves.* ROBIN *takes the record out of the package and puts it on the phonograph. It is Carmen Miranda singing "South American Way".* ROBIN *walks to the window, looks at the street, then turns back and listens to the record. Blackout.*]

            "South American Way" merges with the cry from the minaret.

            The lights rise. Late evening.

            The DUCHESS *sits on the chair. Silence.*

            ROBIN *enters the hallway from a bedroom. He is back into Western clothes. He notices a new set of luggage in the hallway. He walks into the sitting room.*

ROBIN   Is that your luggage? In the hallway?

DUCHESS   Yes.

ROBIN   Are you leaving?

DUCHESS   Yes. Later.

ROBIN   Where?

DUCHESS   Palestine. I have a pass.

ROBIN   For the midnight train?

DUCHESS   For the midnight train. Does that surprise you? I do not think it does.

ROBIN   How?

DUCHESS   Horatio. He came to my room one hour ago. He had the pass in his hand. He said he had worried about me, he had worried all day, he could not eat.

ROBIN   Goodness.

DUCHESS   He knew he had to help me. He was so worried his face took on spots. He had a fever.

ROBIN   Poor Horatio.

DUCHESS   He begged the Embassy for a pass.

ROBIN   That was extremely nice of him.

DUCHESS   It was. Extremely. Only there is no truth in it at all.

ROBIN   What do you mean?

DUCHESS   This man does not do extremely nice things. So? I think perhaps you had a finger in this? Or Emily?

ROBIN   Take the ticket, Duchess, and . . .

DUCHESS   Do not ask questions. Yes, I know the rules. Well, if, if not, thank you anyway.

ROBIN   I suppose you are welcome, anyway.

> [*The lights suddenly go out. The room is completely black.*]

DUCHESS   Ah. The power again.

ROBIN   Damn.

[*The lights come back on.*]

ROBIN   This will go on all night. I think it's a hint. We should have blackouts, you know. We should use no electricity at night. But Cairo's not that sort of city. Blackouts would be useless anyhow. Enemy planes can always follow the Nile. You will be safer in Palestine.

DUCHESS   There is one problem.

ROBIN   What?

DUCHESS   I am so tired.

ROBIN   You've been searching for a pass all day long.

DUCHESS   Yes, I know.

ROBIN   And now you have it.

DUCHESS   And now I don't want it. Yes. Of course. [*Pause.*] I do not want to move again.

ROBIN   But the Germans?

DUCHESS   So? So let them find me.

ROBIN   But they may kill you.

DUCHESS   So? So let them.

ROBIN   You're talking rubbish.

DUCHESS   I tell you the truth about Anna.

ROBIN   Who is Anna?

DUCHESS   My love.

ROBIN   You said her name was Sophia.

DUCHESS   Did I?

ROBIN   Yes. Sophia.

DUCHESS   Fancy that. Sophia. That's not a Jewish name. [*Pause.*] I lied.

ROBIN   Why did you lie?

DUCHESS   Why should I tell the truth?

ROBIN   I believed you.

DUCHESS   Because it was not incorrect. [*Pause.*] I be-
            trayed her.

ROBIN   Anna?

DUCHESS   Yes, Anna, of course. The Gestapo stopped us in
            Cologne.

ROBIN   Cologne?

DUCHESS   Anna was German. She thought we'd be safer
            there. Logic doesn't enter into it. At any rate,
            we did not have papers. I betrayed her.

ROBIN   How?

DUCHESS   With my eyes. I looked at the officer, and my
            eyes said, speak to her first. Not me. Her. And
            he did, and as he did, Anna made a drama. I
            knew she would make a drama to save me, and
            I ran, I escaped. I heard Anna screaming. I
            heard gunshots. My eyes betrayed her.

ROBIN   Not really.

DUCHESS   Yes — really. This I carry with me all my life. I
            am tired of carrying. I did not want to die.
            When I looked at the officer, I did not want to
            die. I'd rather Anna died. But Anna was my
            life. You see, it is simple — I chose to live,
            which meant living a life without the one
            person I could not live without. I do not
            understand anything. I am so tired. To take a
            train once again. Into another country, once
            again. Someplace else, once again.

ROBIN   I saw your future, do you remember?

DUCHESS   Another life.

ROBIN   Yes.

DUCHESS   But that was with Sophia. There was no Sophia.

ROBIN   The name wasn't important.

DUCHESS   No.

ROBIN   I went through too much to get this pass, Duchess.

DUCHESS   Ah. So it *was* you. Not him.

ROBIN   Not him.

DUCHESS   As I thought.

ROBIN   Take the train.

DUCHESS   Do you go someplace else as well?

ROBIN   Yes.

DUCHESS   Do you want to?

ROBIN   No.

DUCHESS   Ah.

ROBIN   And yes. Yes and no.

DUCHESS   But will you go?

ROBIN   I must.

DUCHESS   Then it is as it is then.

ROBIN   What?

DUCHESS   She is here now? Anna? Looking after me?

ROBIN   Yes. I promise.

DUCHESS   Hard to believe. [*Pause.*] I will not miss the train. In case it's true. I will not miss the train.

ROBIN   Good.

DUCHESS   After all, Rommel is almost here.

ROBIN   Tomorrow, certainly.

DUCHESS   I would like to say goodbye to Emily. But
          Horatio said she has left for Alexandria. She
          goes in wrong direction. You and Emily are
          kind to me. I am grateful. [*rises*] Well — I
          return for my luggage. First I must pray.

ROBIN   Pray?

DUCHESS   Speak to some thing I cannot see. If it cannot
          be seen, it must be real. I'll go to the Mosque.

ROBIN   But you're Jewish.

DUCHESS   Yes, and I pretend to be Christian. So — of
          course — I will go to the Mosque.

ROBIN   Of course.

DUCHESS   Now you begin to understand.

          [*The* DUCHESS *goes into the hallway and
          leaves the house.* ROBIN *takes a pear and
          runs his hand over its surface. He does
          the same with an apple.* HORATIO *enters
          the hallway from his bedroom, carrying a
          bottle.*]

ROBIN   Did you ever feel a pear? Feel the shape? Just
          close your eyes . . .

          [HORATIO *enters the sitting room and
          empties the bottle into the earthenware
          jar.*]

HORATIO   This is unreal gin. Straight from Cyprus. God
          knows what's in it. There's no blend. Emily
          knew how to get this right. She had a nose for
          recipes. Very practical. Tahia's not like that at
          all. She doesn't even sew her own costumes,
          unlike almost every other self-respecting belly
          dancer in creation. She's useless. I have no idea

who is going to mix the goula now. [*scoops a cup into the brew*] Want some?

[*He holds out another cup to* ROBIN.]

ROBIN   No. [*Pause.*] Oh, what the hell.

[*He takes the cup from* HORATIO.]

HORATIO   Tahia will be dancing soon.

ROBIN   [*drinks from his cup*] Oh God, this is poison. Are you going?

HORATIO   Where?

ROBIN   To see her dance. You never miss her, do you?

HORATIO   It won't be the same. Something has changed.

ROBIN   What has?

HORATIO   I'm not certain. But now I'm free. [*drinks*] I think Emily used to spice it up a bit — cinnamon or something. Oh, well, nothing's up to scratch, it's wartime, eh? More? [*scoops some more brew from the jar*] Why exactly did you help me?

ROBIN   I wanted a pass for the Duchess.

HORATIO   But you hate me.

[*He refills* ROBIN's *cup.*]

ROBIN   I suppose. Probably. I hate what you've done. But it's done. It was too late to help Emily, but still time to save the Duchess. Simple as that. Make the best of things. Wartime, eh? And you did finally bring the pass.

HORATIO   I did.

ROBIN   So I've managed to accomplish something. [*Pause.*] Was it difficult? The pass?

HORATIO	Not really. But you must have had another motive.
ROBIN	Don't think so.
HORATIO	Perhaps some orange. It needs something. [*squeezes an orange into the jar*] Do you intend to hold it over my head?
ROBIN	What do you mean?
HORATIO	Bring it up again — some day.
ROBIN	Why should I?
HORATIO	Will you control me?
ROBIN	Don't be stupid.
HORATIO	[*throws the orange peel into the jar*] Perhaps this will work. Flowers. What about adding petals? [*takes a rose and pulls the petals off, and throws them into the jar*] Tahia's dancing at this very moment.
ROBIN	You said.
HORATIO	I never miss her.
ROBIN	So go then.
HORATIO	I've lost my appetite. Let's see now . . . [*scoops some more brew into his cup and drinks*] Nothing is mixed correctly. With Emily it was effortless. What do you want from me?
ROBIN	Nothing. Well — actually, I wouldn't mind being alone for a while.
HORATIO	Do you want secrets?
ROBIN	What kind of secrets?
HORATIO	Top secret secrets.
ROBIN	What are you talking about?
HORATIO	Secrets that really are secrets, not secrets that

everyone in Cairo knows. Secrets not even the King's managed to buy. Classified information. The order of battle for the next offensive, as an example.

ROBIN   [*drinking*] The flowers help, actually. Why would I want that?

HORATIO   For your paymasters.

ROBIN   My what?

HORATIO   Your employers.

ROBIN   Who are they?

HORATIO   The Jerries.

ROBIN   Don't be a fool.

HORATIO   They'll be here soon.

ROBIN   I imagine.

HORATIO   I've lost my appetite. I don't see how I can watch Tahia dance any more and concentrate. Her love seems meaningless now. I'm trapped. I'm drowning. I'm in great danger. Are you a spy?

ROBIN   Would I tell you if I was?

HORATIO   No.

ROBIN   So don't ask. I really think you should go and stare at Tahia's belly. It will work miracles. Your appetite will return. I'd like to be alone.

HORATIO   You're a dangerous man. You know too much. I am totally compromised.

ROBIN   I am not a spy, all right? Satisfied? I don't think the goula's good for you.

HORATIO   The Embassy thinks you're a spy. You have no records. Officially, you don't exist. Everything is so lax here, people can say they're anything, half of Cairo is a fraud; but this time I insisted they make a thorough check; after all, I never did believe anything about you. They finally got around to it and of course there isn't any you.

ROBIN   My goodness! No me?

HORATIO   No. Nada. Nein. Just tell me — are you an employee of the Germans or are you yourself a Hun?

ROBIN   Do you really care?

HORATIO   Only insofar as it concerns me. You have a hold over me.

ROBIN   That's a song title. You talk in song titles.

HORATIO   You're a dangerous man.

ROBIN   You said that. Go away, Horatio. I'm tired of this.

HORATIO   No.

> [HORATIO *walks to the table, opens the drawer, and removes a pistol. He points it at* ROBIN.]

ROBIN   Oh dear.

HORATIO   I've spent the last hour thinking.

ROBIN   That's not good.

HORATIO   I'm in serious trouble. As long as you're alive.

ROBIN   Oh do put that thing away. Have another drink.

HORATIO   If I shot a spy, I'd be a hero . . .

ROBIN   Oh Gawd.

HORATIO   Especially a spy who has murdered my wife.

ROBIN   Oh that's a nice touch.

HORATIO   You are bad news, I'm afraid.

ROBIN	Put it away. It doesn't suit you.
HORATIO	Even your boyfriend thinks you're a secret agent.
ROBIN	That's not true.
HORATIO	He told me so.
ROBIN	Nonsense.
HORATIO	His superiors informed him. He's not aware of it, of course, but that's why they're sending him into the desert. He is, after all, a fairly useless officer. They're hoping he'll cop it.
ROBIN	Do you really mean that?
HORATIO	I don't say what I don't mean.
ROBIN	How can you be so cruel?
HORATIO	What?
ROBIN	You fools . . .
HORATIO	So he knows all about you.
ROBIN	He only has a few hours to live. He mustn't die thinking I'm a traitor. You fools.
HORATIO	How do you know?
ROBIN	Know what?
HORATIO	That he has a few hours to live.
ROBIN	You said it yourself. They hope he won't make it.
HORATIO	Yes — but a few hours?
ROBIN	I see the future.
HORATIO	You're mental.
ROBIN	I see the future. Sometimes. In bits and pieces. I have to do a little routine. But it works.

HORATIO You're not merely a German spy, you're a demented German spy as well. And I allowed myself to fall into your hands. I cannot believe I was so careless. It's because Emily muddled my mind. Emily confused me. Emily led me into a snake pit. I can be led by other people so easily. Well, no more. For once in my life I'm going to think of myself and shoot you.

ROBIN You mustn't do that.

HORATIO Everyone's doing it to everyone else in the desert. I can do it in town.

ROBIN Just put it away. Do you know anything about guns?

HORATIO This isn't my first war.

ROBIN It doesn't seem to be your war at all.

HORATIO I was in the last one. One was enough. Most of my friends died. I used one of these.

ROBIN It might go off.

HORATIO When I pull the trigger.

ROBIN I promise — promise — you I am not a spy. And yes — OK, OK — I am not a reporter either. That was fairly obvious. And — OK, OK — I'm not from New Zealand. I'm not from Germany . . . I'm not . . . Oh forget it . . . Just throw that silly thing away. It's time for me to go anyhow.

HORATIO Go?

ROBIN Home.

HORATIO Ah. And where is that?

ROBIN Someplace else entirely.

HORATIO Where?

ROBIN   I can't tell you.

HORATIO   Fine. Time to shoot you.

ROBIN   I'm not supposed to tell you. I'm not supposed to tell anyone. The awful thing is I've wanted to tell someone all day, but not at gunpoint. I wanted to tell the Duchess. I almost did. Actually, when people ask, I do sometimes say it, quickly, in passing. I said it to you this morning. You laughed.

HORATIO   What are you babbling about?

ROBIN   You see . . . perhaps you should sit down . . . well, if you're holding a pistol, I suppose it feels better standing, more masculine . . . You see . . . what I actually am, in fact, in truth, oddly enough, strange though it may seem . . . oh dear, I hope you don't laugh; people shoot those things off by accident while they're laughing . . . what I actually am is a person — well, no, strictly speaking, not a person — a "being" rather, or the word you all seem to prefer, a creature, yes a creature, a creature from another world, someplace else, another planet, a creature from what you term outer space.

HORATIO   You're right. I will sit down.

ROBIN   Obviously I don't look like this at home. I have another form entirely, in my reality, although I'm nothing like the ridiculous fantasies you have on this planet. What I mean is, I am not green. That really upsets me, and it's very important for you to know that. I'm orange, actually. A kind of orange. I'm a two foot orange blob, with an intelligence you cannot even begin to dream of, although the great irony is, in my world I'm thought to be quite stupid, almost a retard.

HORTATIO   You're barking.

ROBIN   This is supposed to be a holiday — that's the joke of it all — a holiday — can you imagine?

HORATIO   You're several degrees beyond barking. Perhaps I should simply tell the police you're a madman — well, it won't be the police, will it — it will be our chaps — but if I say you're crackers and that's why you murdered my wife, it shouldn't be at all difficult to find witnesses to testify that you're gaga.

ROBIN   It's the way we take a holiday. We sit at home, and with instructions, with the proper aid, we are able to project ourselves into another world, into another skin. I'm really back home watching myself here at this very moment. Whatever do you suppose I'm thinking? It's only a short stay, we only ever come for a short stay, unlike other planets, who take it very seriously and do an entire life. The problem is, the brochures did not advertise emotions. Well, they couldn't, I suppose . . . we don't have a word for emotion. I wish I had never come. Some frigging holiday! But you see, there is this pain in my heart. What a foolish people you are. Of course, if I hadn't come, I would never have heard music. Or touched Alec. It's his arms, his upper arms, just beneath the shoulder, that fill me with lust. Lust! I hate my thoughts. How can you people feel two things at the same time, two conflicting things? Or even more? Or anything, for that matter. I want to go back home. I don't want to go back home. Look, darling, please put that evil thing down. There's a technicality you see. If we meet an unnatural death on our short visit here, we are not allowed to reassemble properly; I can't begin to explain it, just take my word. I won't be able to go back; nor will I be able to stay here; I'll just float for ever. Don't do that to me. I think they probably expect that to happen back there, knowing I'm stupid. Don't do that to me.

[*Pause.*]

HORATIO   I don't want you to call me darling.

ROBIN   Sorry.

HORATIO   Alien creatures do not call earthlings darling. People from another planet are not louche, Kiwi homosexuals. Well, you're not Kiwi. What am I talking about?

ROBIN   I know this is out of the ordinary.

HORATIO   This has been a frightful day.

ROBIN   We never know in advance what form we'll take. I don't think I've done at all badly. I'm rather dishy by your standards, don't you think?

HORATIO   I feel dizzy. And it's not just the goula.

ROBIN   Throw the pistol away.

HORATIO   You must think I'm an absolute fool. Everyone thinks I'm a fool. Emily thought I was a fool. I wouldn't be surprised if Tahia does as well; sometimes her smile is a half-smile. I'm not ever certain if she's loving me or laughing at me. How are you supposed to tell the difference? But not even Emily would have dared to tell me an outrageous story like yours.

ROBIN   Why is it so difficult to believe? If you have no trouble at all accepting that a virgin can give birth, and that the father was an unseen spirit, and that the child of this bizarre union is able eventually to walk on water, cure lepers and the lame, restore a blind man's sight, turn

water into wine, and most impressively, feed
thousands of people with only a few loaves of
bread, not to mention resurrecting himself after
he has been killed, why can't you believe that
I'm a two foot orange blob? What is wrong with
you?

[HORATIO *rises. He is unsteady.*]

HORATIO   I don't feel at all well.

ROBIN   You poor thing . . .

HORATIO   I have a fever again.

ROBIN   I'll phone a doctor.

HORATIO   My forehead is burning.

ROBIN   Let me go to Madame Badia's.

HORATIO   Why?

ROBIN   I'll bring Tahia.

HORATIO   You don't believe me. Touch my forehead.

[ROBIN *stares at him.*]

Go ahead. Touch it.

[HORATIO *waves the pistol at* ROBIN, *who
walks to* HORATIO *and reaches for his
forehead.*]

ROBIN   [*motions toward the pistol*] That thing is in the
way.

HORATIO   Touch it!

[ROBIN *feels* HORATIO's *forehead.*]

Well?

ROBIN   Yes.

HORATIO   See!

ROBIN   It's burning.

HORATIO	I knew it! It happens when I'm around lunatics. It's because I am basically so sane, and people like me should never be exposed to anyone off-centre. Emily was mad, you see. I'm very aware of that in retrospect. All right, I confess, I lost my balance over Tahia. Well, that's human, how can you blame me? Perhaps you did as well. Over Alec. Perhaps you have a fever as well.
ROBIN	That's another issue.
HORATIO	No. It isn't. I can understand that. Let me feel your forehead.
ROBIN	Put the pistol away.
HORATIO	Bend down.
ROBIN	This is beside the point.
HORATIO	Bend down!
ROBIN	[*bends his head toward* HORATIO] Don't let your finger slip.
HORATIO	[*feels* ROBIN's *forehead*] Yes, yes, it's burning.
ROBIN	Yes.
HORATIO	We're both burning. You for an upper arm, me for a belly, we're both absolute fools. But then, if I shoot you, my fever will disappear.
ROBIN	That doesn't follow.
HORATIO	Instinct. I must shoot you.
ROBIN	What is so difficult? I really don't understand. Why is it impossible to accept anything outside your normal range of thinking?
HORATIO	I don't want to hear any more of this nonsense. I'm not burning up because of love.
ROBIN	You said you were.

HORATIO I didn't mean what I said. Obviously, I didn't mean what I said. Why isn't Emily here to clarify things?

ROBIN You killed her, actually.

HORATIO Don't try to confuse me. It's fear. I'm afraid of what you know.

ROBIN But I will have disappeared within the hour. My holiday is over. I have to go back, no matter what. I can't be a danger to you if I'm not here. Think it through. You don't have to shoot me.

HORATIO That would be true if it were true, but it's not true.

ROBIN Huh?

HORATIO Do you expect me to believe you?

ROBIN You accept electricity. What the hell is electricity? Can you please explain a telephone? How is it possible to hear a person talking thousands of miles away? Forget some convoluted scientific explanation that you only pretend to understand, just tell me how it's possible. Or radio. How can you turn on a switch and hear Vera Lynn in Cairo when Vera Lynn is actually in London? Would you have believed any of that a few hundred years ago? How does a camera preserve an image? If these things are possible, why am I not possible, then?

HORATIO I'm pointing a pistol at you. And I'm about to shoot it. This is not an intellectual act. I've been slow, I agree, but then it's difficult to do this sort of thing point-blank. It isn't easy for me to assert myself; I have to work up to it. But I am going to kill you, I promise you that. I'm saving my skin. That's what matters to me. I have no desire to see beyond that. It's very simple. There's no philosophy involved. I have a fever and I want it to go away.

ROBIN Aren't you curious?

HORATIO About what?

ROBIN About me. About my life at home. About my world.

HORATIO No.

ROBIN You must be.

HORATIO I'm not even curious about this world. Do you think I was thinking about Rommel in the desert or the Japanese in Mandalay when I was kissing Tahia?

ROBIN Don't do this.

HORATIO I must. Walk back a bit.

ROBIN Why?

HORATIO I need distance. You're too close. This is too personal.

ROBIN Why should I walk back? You walk back.

HORATIO Oh. Fair enough.

[HORATIO *takes a few steps backwards.*]

ROBIN I'm begging you. You've succeeded in degrading me, if that gives you any pleasure. I'm actually begging you.

HORATIO Oh, look, if you really are a little orange person with a superior brain, then find a way to stop me. Surely you must possess extraordinary powers that we poor little earth things know nothing about. So stop me. Or shut up.

ROBIN I can't.

HORATIO Then I'm sorry, old chap, but this is finally it.

ROBIN   You see, it hurts my head.

HORATIO   What does?

ROBIN   Using my powers. It gives me a terrible headache.

HORATIO   You really are good value. I hate to do this.

ROBIN   It gives me little shooting pains in my brain. And ringing in my ears. I'd rather reason with you.

HORATIO   You can't reason with a fever. Haven't you learnt that? Life was totally uncomplicated a few hours ago. Yes, it is true, of course, that Tahia was also sleeping with Siree Pasha, but he's one of the King's closest advisers, and I accepted that, just as Tahia accepted Emily, there was, after all, a balance; of course, she was also sleeping with Debois from the Free French, but that wasn't a complication. I was in love. It was simple. I was alive. I wasn't afraid. But now I'm burning. I must be free. I'm sorry.

        [HORATIO *steadies his pistol and aims at* ROBIN's *heart.* ROBIN *presses his palms against his head.*]

ROBIN   Ouch! Damn it! I hate this!

HORATIO   I want the burning to stop.

ROBIN   [*pressing tighter*] Ouch! Damn it! Shit!

HORATIO   Goodbye.

        [HORATIO *pulls the trigger, but as he does, the pistol bends in his hand, and slowly melts away.* HORATIO *stares at it in disbelief.*]

What's happening?

ROBIN   I can't tell you how much this hurts.

          [HORATIO *moves forward, then stops, and
          shivers. He feels his body.*]

HORATIO   I'm cold.

          [*The grandfather clock begins to chime,
          and the hands on the clock start to
          revolve wildly.*]

ROBIN   Oh shit — the fucking clock . . .

          [ROBIN *continues to press his palms
          against his head. The phonograph begins
          to play "South American Way" in triple
          time. A piano rolls into the hallway from
          a bedroom, scales playing by themselves,
          then rolls back. Liquid shoots out of the
          earthenware jar.*]

HORATIO   I'm freezing. Emily — what's happening?

          [*Icicles shoot out over* HORATIO's *body. He
          stares at* ROBIN, *then slowly sinks to the
          ground.*]

ROBIN   I need an aspirin.

          [ROBIN *removes his hands from his head.
          He looks at* HORATIO, *walks over to his
          body, and gently kicks it. It seems life-
          less.*]

          Well, well, well. "There are more things in
          heaven and earth than are dreamt of in your
          philosophy." Eh, Horatio? [*covers his ears*]
          Shush!

          [*The lights black out. It is completely
          dark.*]

The lights come on again.

The chimes have stopped, as have the hands on the clock, and the music. The jar is still.

ROBIN *is still looking at* HORATIO. HAMID *stands in the doorway.*

HAMID   Entire family dead?

> [HAMID *walks into the room.*]

ROBIN   Hamid.

HAMID   British not wait for Germans. Do it themselves.

ROBIN   You might say.

HAMID   Funny people.

ROBIN   Well, I imagine you'll be rid of them soon.

HAMID   No. Germans not enter Cairo.

ROBIN   You don't have to keep saying that now.

HAMID   It is true. Indeed. We hear stories. Real stories. British winning in desert. At El Alamein. Cairo is safe.

ROBIN   Oh. Yes. Of course.

HAMID   No more papers falling on head. [*looks at* HORATIO] His cards were not good.

ROBIN   He isn't dead. Just in a kind of trance. Here — help me . . .

> [ROBIN *takes* HORATIO's *shoulders;* HAMID *grabs his legs; they pick him up.*]

On the couch.

> [*They place* HORATIO *on the couch.*]

Now this . . .

> [ROBIN *moves the screen around the couch, hiding it from view.*]

Now, Hamid, I have a favour to ask. Will you have your friends bring Mrs Walker's body back and place it on the floor where it was. And return the knife as well, but put it into Mr Walker's hand. He won't wake up until tomorrow. Poor baby, he'll have a sore throat. I don't know what he'll tell the police. He can try the one about a man from outer space. Actually, if I know my Horatio, he'll talk his way out of it. So be it. Whatever. Although if he just can't manage it and they actually execute him, I've done him an enormous favour. His soul will be free to return almost immediately, and if it takes human form, he will reach maturity in an age when selfishness is truly appreciated. [*looks behind screen*] You have a future yet, old chap! [*turns to* HAMID] Then after, go to my room; there's a lot of money there; please take it for yourself and your friends.

HAMID   You will not need it?

ROBIN   No.

HAMID   You go away?

ROBIN   Yes, Hamid.

HAMID   Indeed. [*Pause.*] I have seen you before.

ROBIN   Me?

HAMID   No. Yours.

ROBIN   [*smiles*] Oh.

HAMID   They always sing at Pyramids.

ROBIN   Yes.

HAMID   Salaam, my friend.

ROBIN   Salaam.

[HAMID *leaves. The lights black out. It is completely dark.*]

The lights come on again.

ROBIN *is holding a lemon and feeling its contours. He cuts the lemon open. He squeezes its juice into his mouth. He looks around the room. He touches bits and pieces in the room.*

ROBIN   Oh Alec, it's the top of your arms. And it's Carmen Miranda. And it's jasmine. And the sea. And traffic. And Mozart. And the white moon over Cairo. And regret. Once we return, all memory of the holiday is erased. Not even to know that I've forgotten! Perhaps there will be a nagging feeling somewhere at the edge of my soul. Feeling. [*Pause.*] Feeling!

                    [*The lights black out. It is completely dark.*]

The lights come on again.

ROBIN, *as we know him, has disappeared. In his place is a two foot orange blob that pulsates on the floor. It makes strange little electronic noises. It flies out of the window.*

The lights black out. It is completely dark.

There is the sound of a door opening, the sound of someone in the hallway.

A match is lit. The DUCHESS *holds the match. She walks into the sitting room.*

The lights come on again. The room is empty, except for the DUCHESS. *The* DUCHESS *looks around.*

DUCHESS   Hello? No one is here?

[*The* DUCHESS *walks to the window. She opens the shutters. She looks out onto the street, then up at the sky.*]

Oh — a shooting star!
[*sings*] "Twinkle, twinkle little star
How I wonder who you are."
[*closes her eyes*] Now make a wish. Yes. Right.
[*opens her eyes*] Oh! Pish! What is wrong with me? To still hope. Ach! Take the train.

[*The* DUCHESS *starts towards the hallway. Suddenly she looks at the floor and screams.*]

Oh my God!

[*The* DUCHESS *runs around the room in a frenzy.*]

The shit! The shit!

[*The* DUCHESS *gathers her courage, and stamps on the floor with her shoe, closing her eyes as she does.*]

There.

[*The* DUCHESS *opens her eyes. She takes a piece of paper from the table and removes something from the bottom of her shoe.*]

Damned cockroach!

[*She throws the paper out of the window. She walks into the hallway, takes her luggage, and leaves.*]

The End